GW01091383

ANCHOR BOOKS

POEMS FROM THE

SOUTH EAST

First published in Great Britain in 1995 by
ANCHOR BOOKS
1-2 Wainman Road, Woodston,
Peterborough, PE2 7BU

All Rights Reserved

Copyright Contributors 1995

HB ISBN 1 85930 263 7
SB ISBN 1 85930 268 8

Foreword

Anchor Books is a small press, established in 1992, with the aim of promoting readable poetry to as wide an audience as possible.

We hope to establish an outlet for writers of poetry who may have struggled to see their work in print.

The poems presented here have been selected from many entries. Editing proved to be a difficult and daunting task and as the Editor, the final selection was mine.

The poems chosen represent a cross-section of styles and content. They have been sent from all over the world, written by young and old alike, united in the passion for writing poetry.

I trust this selection will delight and please the authors and all those who enjoy reading poetry.

Glenn Jones
Editor

CONTENTS

THE DISAPPOINTMENT

We took Auntie to see
Regents Park on Sunday afternoon;
We showed her the Queen Mary beds-
The roses were in bloom.

People taking photographs;
Cricket on the green,
But Auntie said, There isn't
Any antirrhinum to be seen.

In Bridlington, they have a really
Wonderful display; varieties, dwarf
Yellow and my favourite - maroons,
Like lovely velvet lining in
A box of silver spoons.

Look at the geraniums and jacaranda
Ferns, John Major's blue delphiniums
And poppies, Labour red.
Where are the snapdragons, Are there none,
Auntie Doris said.

A wee bit disappointed,
Auntie returned for tea, and
Taking doughnuts from the doily,
Pronounced reconcilingly,
The violas were pretty, and of course
We all agreed.

Marianne Barber

1

MY VILLAGE

I came to this village
When I was ten,
'Tween the downs and
The sea. And then
Who would have thought
It would change so much,
No little cottages
Graced with thatch.
No clear roads
With a horse to catch!
The one village shop
Has long since gone.
Now supermarkets reign
Alright for some.
The fields have all gone
We have houses galore
And by what I hear,
There may be more.
My little green village
Is fading away.
But the pub and the church
Managed to stay!
Now, the old ones say
Oh! For the days
When life was slower
Before we had this thing
Called power!
Were it to stop
Would the world stop too?
I wonder wouldn't you!

H M Cobby

THE OUTING

'What's it like at Camber Sands? Do tell us please, Grandma.'
Excitedly they clap their hands. 'Is it very far?'

I do recall those summer days
When my three girls were small.
Driving down the Kent highways
Where Camber would enthral
Them with its golden beach
And miles of paddling room.
So many shells, plenty for each
To pick and choose. And for whom
It was a treat
To pack a picnic meal.
Delicious things for them to eat.
The memory is so real.

We sometimes went on winter days
The wind could be so strong,
It whipped the water into sprays
Which chased us all along
The empty sands. We whooped with glee
Holding fast to swirling kites
Pulling towards the sea.
Keeping dogs within our sights
Lest they should run to find
Adventures new. That salty tang,
All brings to mind
The homeward songs we sang.

'Shall we go to Camber Sands? Please take us there Grandma.'
Into mine they slip their hands. 'Let's go there in your car.'

Diana Dixon

AUTUMN

It was one of those late October days,
With an Indian summer haze.
That hang like a shroud o'er the countryside
Spreading beauty far and wide.

Murmuring gently the wood-scented breeze,
Shimmering sunbeams drift through the trees.
Autumn tints, fields of shining gold.
Harvests riches of bounty unfold.

Warm lies the earth, the magic spell grows,
Cherish each moment as the evening sun glows.
Peace and contentment descends over all
Inspiring is autumn in the fall.

G Craigie

WHITSTABLE

What was it about you that drew me ever on
To move here when my working days were done.
I first stayed here in nineteen fifty-two
But never knew I'd end up loving you,
Your old world charm, your air of mystery
Engendered by the alleys to the sea.
To walk along the shore where others past have trod
Greeted with a smile, a warm and friendly nod
From other people that I do not know,
They warm my heart and make my spirit glow
And on the bench where Peter Cushing sat
Old friends now sit to enjoy a little chat.
On shopping days there is a lively bustle
But not a shove or push, or angry hustle
And shop assistants give a friendly smile
No-one complains if you stand and talk a while.
I live here now and with contented sigh
Will stay here, happy, 'til the day I die.

Olive Wallis

MY HOME IN THE SOUTH

I was born in the south
With a silver spoon in my mouth
I have travelled around and overseas
To places of beauty but wherever I stray
Nowhere pleases me in the same old way
The garden of England, Kent has been called
But the beauty of Sussex can be seen by all
It is always good to be home again
Where my roots are set and I will ever remain
Spending my days where I was born
Hearing the birds in the early morn
Where the air is fresh and clean
And the best of nature can be seen
Each season has it's special beauty
Creating landscapes that can be ·
Captured with artists brush and paint
Little villages so quaint
There is a lot to be said for the Country life
Tramping through forests, husband and wife
Breathing in the pinewood smells
Beech trees with sun streaming through to the dells
Beautiful carpets of aromatic bluebells
Purples and mauves of thick heath and heather
I know, that wherever I go, I will never
Find the natural beauty that I call home
I am wholly contented and no longer will roam.

Evelyn A Evans

SNOW AND A SUNSET

How beautiful the earth doth look
When carpeted with snow,
The finest wonder of the world-
Minutest flakes we know.

Intense the stillness in the air
As white flakes drift around,
The sun makes sparkle, snowballs start,
Toboggans then abound.

These crystals in the vast unknown,
Were fashioned long ago.
Science, skill, were needed not
To make these specks of snow.

Then on our homeward journey
We came through cast of Rye,
There we beheld the glory of
A most fantastic sky.

This brilliance of a sunset,
Against the bare stark trees
The horizon - oh, so wonderful
Man takes God's gifts - no fees.

The wonders of the planets,
The gold in rays of sun,
But the glories of a sunset
Surpass them - everyone.

Dorothy Cousins

ROCHESTER UPON MEDWAY-CITY OF DICKENS

When tourists talk they mention Canterbury
Or York, or London, where they made merry.
But more and more now tell the tale
Of Rochester, 'gainst which other cities pale.
We cross over Medway's swirling waters
And see a high street filled with laughter
Where people walk with costumes colourful
All gaily dressed for Dickens's Festival.
'Neath famous clock they march with pride
With Dickens's memories close beside.
Old Bill Sykes passes six poor travellers
Even his dog joins with the revellers
And crowds come in from far and wide
To see the show and more beside
For from lofty castle's ramparts
They see it all when procession starts.
First Mr Pickwick with his club
His characters, the one we love
Oh yes, there's even Nancy
I guess Bill Sykes she's sure to fancy.
Now Fagin passes with his poor lads
They stride along clad in their rags
Each year it comes, filled with pride
Dickens' lovers we're all inside
Rochester citizens we're glad to be
So much to do, so much to see.
And off the high street there's restaurant fare
We wine and dine in comfort there
Now evening's come, the day soon ends
Farewell fair city from your new friends.

Cyril Saunders

MY BEDROOM WINDOW VIEW...

I awake quite alert with the light of the sun
A new day ahead and new things begun
But all of a sudden I jump up in fright
- It's then that I realise there's something not right
I open my curtains as quiet as a mouse
And see that some builders are making a house.
But as I look closer they're not making *one*
I soon start to see that there's *several* to come!
I stand there in shock, this change is so soon,
And then, even worse, they can see in my room!
You'd think from the noise they were starting a riot,
They're not even trying in the least to be quiet.
Gone are the flowers, and the big oak tree
Now it's the bricks and the rubble I see
I shut tight my curtains, and sit on my bed
- I wonder if *I* should be moving instead?

Gail Bromham

FOOTPATH 239, PEMBURY

For years, and years,
These trees have stood,
The trials of time and tide.
Silently they stand aloof,
Like giants above so high.
They've out lived
Landings on the moon,
Dictatorships, Queens and Kings,
For decades yet, they'll still be there,
Well in the 21st century.
And if you travel along 239,
The footpath rugged and old,
Deep down below the Pembury vales,
Come sleet, or snow, or cold-
'Tis then you'll feel or sense some time,
As in the days of yore,
When villagers still walked this way
A thousand times before.

Terrence St John

COLDRED, B.K.V....!

Kent, Garden of England, yields a fair harvest.
Small towns and villages thrive on the chalk.
On breezy uplands, and nestling in valleys,
Flocks of fat sheep, Kentish plovers, and hawk.

Roman and Saxon have all made their home here.
One special Hamlet stands out from the rest.
Coldred: whose heritage goes beyond Doomsday,
With farms, church and manors, counted Kent's best!

The Pond on the green could tell some sad stories.
Three centuries past, a poor *witch* was swum.
Longevity's counted as Coldred' best asset,
Along with fine root crops, and *The Carpenters* rum!

An old Saxon church along leaf bordered lanes,
Cottage gardens all blooming, hard work well spent.
The powers that be conferred with each other,
And our village was voted *Best Kept in East Kent!*

Marjorie Chapman

EAST SUSSEX

Although I live in Sussex
I'm as Scottish as can be
Must say I like this county though
With its townships by the sea
I go home to see my kin folk
And I wear my kilt with pride
I love the glens and mountains,
Sometimes wish that I could bide
But in historic Hastings
Is where I've hung my hat
King William and brave Harold
Battle Abbey and all that
Along the road the port of Rye
And its quaint old fashioned shops,
With its cobbled streets and ancient quay
It pulls out all the stops
To attract as many visitors
And tourists as it can
It sometimes leaves old Hastings
To be an *also ran*
But I am not complaining
This cinque port is my home
I do enjoy the sunny south
So perhaps I'll no more roam

Cathie Bridger

SANDWICH

During the middle ages
Sandwich was a chief port,
And the beaten wall at Richborough
Was once a Roman fort.

The narrow lanes of Sandwich
Have a picturesque appeal,
This small town oozes charm
With a quaint and friendly feel.

The streets are medieval
Houses built with brick and wood,
Follow the Bulwarks and Rope walk
Where the old town walls once stood.

A town untouched by change,
Left as a monument to the past
A reminder, of those busy days
When this port ran fierce and fast.

Sarah Maycock

CAMBER, AT A DISTANCE

And the strip of sand lies
Silently, brilliantly in the deep-
Blue sea-
Waiting?
     The seagulls mew to
Spy it new and naked there.-
Waiting? (facing the deep-blue sky
the most perfect eye of God.)
The surface dries and yellows
Acute and distressed-
Waiting?
The deep-blue sea licks and laps
At its hard sides, deliciousness,-
Not long?
     Wettened the sand lies and
Disappears beneath the wash
of
  time.

L Brown

ANITA

The first fluttering of life heralded a brand new dawn
So, I painstakingly prepared for the day you'd be born
At last, I was a mother-to-be, my dream had come true
A miracle had happened
That miracle was you

Through the ensuing months, you and I were one
The thread of life I held so dear
This tiny soul
Which was to become
My daughter, or my son

You came into the world on a sunny August day
A blonde, blue-eyed baby girl
A gift from heaven
So beautifully formed
And perfect in every way

The years have rolled by, and now you're grown
With tender loving care you bloomed
You are now a young woman
At the peak of your youth
So confident, and mature
With a life of your own

Doreen Atherley

FLUTTERS IN THE CITY

Flutters in the city...
They look so pretty, but nerves are tense
There's no pretence: shares can go up and shares can go down
But flutters in the city are looking so pretty
On the old lady of Threadneedle Street.

Flutters in the city...
The windy, blustery day blows cold comfort
For those who are on a sliding scale:
They came up by rail to watch their shares plummet.
Who will be the next casualty?
There will be no bonanza this Christmas.
But Christmas is still a time for hope
And flutters in the city may auger well
For a white Christmas within the sound of Bow Bells.

Flutters in the city...
Every day it's getting colder (or perhaps it's just I'm getting older)
For only a sprinkling of snowflakes are in evidence-
Though no-one ever forgets that childhood thrill.
Seasonal, expensive Christmas cards
Sent from one business executive to another
Illustrate just what I mean:-
Famous city buildings within a snowy scene.

Flutters in the city...
Take a walk - no matter what the weather-
Through the city just before Christmas...
In the deep mid-winter and *upon Westminster Bridge*
Earth has not anything to show more fair
Than Christmas lights on stately old buildings
Contrasting ironically with ancient monuments to Mammon.

Elaine Hunt

ASPECTS OF KENT

Apple orchards and cherries too
Blossom drift in snow-like hue
The Medway rambles to the sea
All Kent's history here to see
Castles, parks, busy towns
Our eyes we lift towards the Downs
Le shuttle goes beneath the sea
A wonder to the world (and me)
On the border Gatwick lies
That flies us off into the skies
Coastal towns with varied shores
Ports, with ferries and hydrofoils
Kent the *GLORY* of the south
So raise your glass
To our country's wealth

B Laxton

CLIMBING THE DOWNS ABOVE EASTBOURNE

A steep and chalky path leads to the Downs
Polished and channelled by the winter rain,
Later it widens to a grassy slope
Where climbing still we look back to the plain.

Now lies the city all spread out below
Like a child's toy, the houses, roads and shops.
A brightly coloured bus runs silently
Along a tiny road. A toy train stops

Beyond the town the sea lies tender blue,
The cliffs and bays and other towns.
We feel a little like Olympic Gods
When we have climbed the summit of the Downs

But when we reach the top we turn away
From noise and stress and all the things that pass,
And hear instead the sound of high lark song,
The peaceful sighing wind in long dry grass.

Irene Wilkins

THE AVENUE

The avenue wherein I dwell
Was once a Peyton Place
Throughout the years there's really been
Some arsenic and old lace

There was the woman up the road
Who felt she'd have no more
Then drained a flask of Lysol
And yelled 'Murder!' from her door

Next door lived the spinster
To church she also ran
But spent her week days scheming
Some vicious evil plan

Then came the war, the church bells tolled
The Nazi 'planes were humming
And Annie stood with sand and hoe
Cos 'Parachutes were coming!'

The heyday of the avenue
Was the gory killing
Of another nagging wife
For gossips all quite thrilling

Some whispered there was 'more to it'
They added bits like 'rape'
This all had the right effect
It made the neighbours gape

Such things today are not so rare
For common are riots and mobs
The Avenue is silent now
And inflation's cooled the snobs

Yoni

19

ROOTED AT WORTHING

Long years ago in London,
And wishing to make a change,
We went to a friendly house agent,
Who had an endless range,
Of houses, flats and mansionettes,
So many, but not to fit the bill!
We had ideas, but could not get
Something, in surroundings different, and yet?
The agent said, 'Just a suggestion
Why not by the sea, for instance Worthing.'
Nice bright town, without question.
With all facilities, plus the lovely Downs
You have just everything on reflection!
With many thanks, so we took wing
In a few days, away to Worthing by the Sea.
Finding, a new home that waited.
How lucky could one be.
With no regrets, our wandering abated,,
At Worthing - now rooted are we.

Madeline Chase Thomas

UNTITLED

Come to the seaside even now it's so bleak
See all the seagulls swooping down at your feet
See all the waves splashing high on the sand
Watching the sea where there is no land
Come in the summer when the crowds fill our town
Stand at the cliff-top, on people look down
Charles Dickens' town that's what we are
Come here by train or maybe by car
There's not much for youngsters apart from our sand
But pubs, parks and cafes you will think grand
We are right on the corner, we are Thanet you know
We sometimes miss rainstorms and also the snow
Walks will delight you there's towns either side
There's Ramsgate and Margate you won't need a guide
So I'll leave my good wishes and hope you will find
Broadstairs comes to you when a holiday's in mind.

Hazel Bowman

CRICKET AT FINDON

Was it not sweet to spring thus on the green,
To fix the eye unerring on the ball;
Between the overs glance upon the scene
Or listen, eager for one's partner's call?

Was it not good to feel reviving skill,
To know the mastery of hand and eye?
Surely the aptitude would be there still
If quite so many years had not gone by?

Was it not grand to share the summer air
With those with whom one's mind was in accord,
To bask or shelter, or just stand and stare,
And sometimes change the numbers on the board?

Was it not fine to clutch the flying ball,
And hear the plaudits ripple round the ground?
Was it not joy to just be there at all,
To relish each delight of sight and sound?

Is it not bitter-sweet to sit at ease
While those one taught, old cricket's craft display?
Perhaps it is eternal youth one sees,
Not just the ghosts of many a yesterday.

John A Nye

ALBION, BLIND ALBION

Oh Albion, blind Albion,
Your lights have been put out,
Quite gone your ornamental hue,
That ghastly, flaky, peeling blue;
Instead you wear a pallid paste,
An ochreous tint that's yellow based,
And dark grey boards have filled your eyes,
Which no longer see the day's sunrise,
That flooded in to greet the sleeping,
Who lay within your walls' safekeeping.

It seems to me your lack of vision,
Reflects somehow the indecision
Shown by this land of ours,
Which once was of the major powers,
That ruled this whirling orb of earth,
That is both grave and place of birth
To countless throngs of human beings:
But unaware of our true mission
We've killed this world with nuclear fission!
And wait our fate as if in prison.

But now blind Albion,
Your body's going too,
For someone's bought you with a view
To make some money from the space,
Which you one hundred and seventy years did grace,
And as with England and its crown,
All that was splendid 'gins to drown
In tears for lost magnificence;
While selfishness and greed doth rule the world
And once smiling lips of love are curled in hate.
God save us all from this cruel fate
Let's hope the flag of truth is soon unfurled.

Anthony Chamberlaine-Brothers

EVENING IN THE PARK

A golden sunset in the west-
The silhouette of silver birch-
Crisp bracken on the hillock crest-
The steeple of a distant church.

'Tis silent but for whispering breeze;
The moon is rising in the sky;
An owl hoots from the old oak trees;
Look! There a stag and deer pass by.
Their movements seem not to disturb
The crisping leaves beneath the brake,
While human footfalls will be heard
By dozing bunnies who'll awake.

Yes, evening in the wooded park
Is truly wondrous to behold,
And, ere the dusk gives place to dark,
A thousand miracles unfold.

J Morris

MY KENTISH HOME

There are oast houses standing all serene
And villages with their tiny streams
Village ponds with resident ducks
And some of the farms with modern trucks.
But my favourite is the great Shire Horse
Who gallops the field with mighty force
With great clods of earth flying from under its feet
For this to me is a rare treat.
For this is their holiday from London Town
After dragging those heavy carts around and around
No wonder they gallop past with glee
For its their yearly holiday and now they are free
It never fails when they gallop joyously by
To bring a tear to my eye.
And let's not forget the quaint old pubs
With seats outside and flowering shrubs
It's like an oasis when one's dry and hot
To find such a pub in a beautiful spot
The peace and tranquillity when one sips their pint
Sitting outside is pure delight.
Then there are the cottages all oak beams and thatch
And a strong front door that once held only a latch
The latch now is just a symbol of bygone days
It's padlocks and bolts now I am sorry to say.
But these old places still have their charm
And give off an atmosphere of peace and calm.
These things I have written I say with pride
Is the beauty of living in our Kent countryside.

Esther Jones

TRAINS PASSING

The eight twenty three, London bound,
High on its embankment, makes the sound
Of a giant's whining toddler as it strains up the hills.
Taking secretaries and managers, and clerks to their tills
In the city, or the West End, or beyond.
Unseeing, they pass the oasts and farmhouse pond,
Their silhouetted heads bowed into their FT
Or Times or Sun... and some, one-time me,
Read and study and shut their eyes to sleep...
Or pray. And merely glance, no, peep
Out the murky glass, to check the morning progress
To London Bridge, or Cannon Street or Charing Cross.
Along the bank the bogies rattle,
Past the uncaring Fresian cattle,
Past the ignoring backs of unshorn ewes
Into the trees and different views.
Now skylarks trill to their place in the sky
And noisy geese honk as they fly
Away from the lake for foreign lands,
Away from the weald to Artic stands.
And, hark, do you hear that whisper?
That building, whistling, bustling, jitter?
Down streaks the eight thirty to Paris:
Sleek and silent and rushing it's harassed
Continentals over the farms,
Over the green fields and the oaken barns,
Away to the tunnel and exotic places.
While we smile, with the sun on our faces;
A walk in the breeze, a chew of a toffee.
We'll be back for ten: it'll be time for coffee!

T F Crockford

DEMOGRAPHIC TIME BOMB?

They say we're all elderly in the South East.
Call us old bats, we don't care in the least,
But the word geriatric is rather unkind.
It suggests we're deficient in body and mind.
I know that, in Crawley, we're not new at all,
But they're glad of our cash in the new shopping mall.

    I do get annoyed when the places we built
    Behave as if living should make us feel guilt.
    I don't need statistics, don't have to be told.
    I can see in my mirror that I'm getting old.
    But it's most reassuring to crones such as me
    There are lines on the rest of the faces I see.

It was perfectly obvious, painfully clear
We were all young together when we moved down here
And, forty years on from pushing the prams
We were bound to end up like over-cooked hams,
But why are we flooded with nursing home offers
With little regard for limited coffers?

    I know that, instead of armies of bikes
    And convoys of pushchairs and skateboards and trikes
    We bumble around on wheelchairs and frames,
    But we're hellishly good at computerised games!
    And we don't need officials or media fusses,
    Just street lights that work and regular buses.

We're not just statistics, we're people as well.
We have worked all our lives and we don't even smell.
We're sponged off, we're taxed, insulted and hurt
The powers-that-be tend to treat us like dirt.
But those that declaim us as well past our best
Forget that, ere long, they'll be old like the rest!

Valerie Johnson

BROADSTAIRS IN WINTER

Little has changed from days of old
When Dickensian feet roamed the cobbled stones
An atmosphere of seasonal gold
Is rampant in the air
The weather is frost cold
My legs have turned blue as mould

The streets are free from waste and litter
There's nothing much to hark
The Christmas tree lights sway and glitter
Home to a nomadic lark
You can stop for chips or chunky pea fritter
On your way to the pub for a pint of bitter

Laura and I share a Chelsea bun
Enjoying the view in the park
The count down to Christmas has just begun
She's shining with youth and expectant fun
If there was a glint of winter sun
We could sit here peacefully till dark.

Janet Oliver

EARLY CLOSING DAY - RAMSGATE

Behind a blank facade
they hide away
Cafe, bookshop, boutique
linked by fate - in checkmate

Once they shut half day
enjoyed a brief respite
Now morning noon and eve
they close, and gently doze

They tried to stay awake
yawned oh so quietly
Used gimmick, free gift
and mammoth sale - to tip the scale

But dreamtime came too soon
and bade them rest
So yawn gave way to sleep
now shuttered eye - greets passers-by

Georgina Cook

MY MOBILE HOME

Our road is a circle
Dwellings each side
Each home a castle
looked after with pride.
Neat curtains and gardens
Some have fence and gate
Each one a number
On wood or brass plate.
Some are double
Some are not
The doubles are roomy
The singles - tight spot.
Hear the rain beat on the roof
Feel the wind when it's strong
Bend the side - though standing firm -
Pray it doesn't last too long.
Come the spring and snowdrops white
Summer and the sunshine bright
See the fields so lush and green
Fruit and veg - the best you've seen
Growing in the smallest plot
With border flowers - yes - the lot.
One day we may move away
From our Home upon the Down
But for now we are content
And treasure our roof as a crown.

Joan Townsend

THE MEMORIAL
CAPEL LE FERNE

A young man sits watching, watching the sea,
Awaiting his buddies, who he'll never see.

He waits there in springtime,
With hope in his eyes,
The summer suns scorch him,
But none heed his sighs.
The autumn soon passes,
With mists, wind and rain,
In winter he's frozen,
Yet he feels no pain.

A young man sits watching, watching the sea,
Remembering his buddies, long gone but free.

Eileen McCappin

CHRISTMAS TREES ON LANGTON GREEN

The butcher's door stands open
Despite the biting air
And the village bakery
Bedecked with lights
Displays its Christmas fare.

The wriggling child smiles
As at the kerb the push-chair stops.
Cocooned in a snowsuit
The young girl points
To the welcoming, beckoning shops.

Past the newsagent and twelve-hour store
Special offers edged in spray-on snow.
No shopping today
The family press on
Past chain-smoking houses, sat proud in a row.

Crossing the turning to Speldhurst
From *The Hare* cheery voices resound
And just beyond
On the edge of the green
Lie rows of trees, strewn on frozen ground.

Twirled round for mother's approval
Boughs shaken and raised to full high.
The young girl shrieks
Her parents laugh
Agreement is reached with her playful delight.

Returning slowly homewards
Father carries their tree shoulder high.
The shop's awning rattles
As pine needles quiver
His daughter's laughter fills the sky.

Peter Cook

ALWAYS THE RIVER

In olden days, when New Road
Was just a dusty track,
Fields and meadows graced the front,
The river graced the back.
The houses nestled side by side,
Where sailors lived in style,
With ship owners and builders
And folk who'd made their pile.
With views across the harbour,
and many a ship to see.
And always, always the river
busily flowing and free.

Where are they now, those sea salts,
And what on earth would they think,
the views blocked out by Parcel Force,
And street lights on the blink.
Where petrol fumes replace the blooms,
New Road's become a car park
No more ships that pass in the night,
But cars that park in the dark.
Fag ends, cartons, empty cans,
To progress we are slaves,
Enough to make those old sea salts
Turn over in their graves . . .

But then was then, and now is now,
And tomorrow's another day,
For there's always, always, the river
And it's definitely here to stay!

Audrey Loftin

PROUD TO BE ROYAL

Have you taken Albert to see Victoria?
It's written on the shopping bags
Did you know that she came here
And everyone waved their flags

When you walk along the Pantiles
Nearing the church of King Charles the Martyr
Think of our royal visitor
And the shopping centre we named after her

See the rocks all made of sandstone
Mount Edgecombe and High Rocks down the road
The ones named after Wellington
And the one that looks like a toad

Take a trip to Happy Valley
Try to find the old Sweeps Cave
Count the steps with a friend
Is the number you reached the same?

Go for a walk in one of the parks
There's Dunorlan and Calverly for a start
Why not sit under the bandstand
And watch as it slowly gets dark

So come spend a day at the Wells
Try looking round our shops   .
Revel in our history
Our town you see is tops

With the serving of spring water
And ringing of our church bells
Can you really, honestly say
You're disgusted of Tunbridge Wells?

James Mankelow

THE CORMORANT

Posing on his winter rock,
The cormorant surveys the world
With wings akimbo.
      Why he does it no one knows.

Lying on our summer beach,
We spread our limbs and watch the rock
Where all the birds stood,
      Remembering their pointless pose.

Brian P Smith

BODIAM CASTLE

With her duck filled moat and turreted towers
Bodiam Castle recalls struggles for power
Nestled in the valley as I approach
No quarter will she give or broach
It is like taking a step back in time
As along the twisting lane I climb
And come face to face with solid walls
A facade, behind is no solidity at all
Just grass and a few crumbling rooms
Not an enemy but neglect her doom
Avoiding the tourists, I sit on my own
To recall knights having to leave this their home
A visitor too yet I do not feel that way
I think of olden times, not present day.

Melanie M Burgess

THE PEOPLE OF LANCING DOWN

Rest awhile and catch your breath, it's been a steepish climb
And let the ghosts of yesterday come back to you in time.
Faintly as a whisper there's the sound of flint and stone,
And you know that in your solitude you're never quite alone.

For on the ridge behind you, the legions marching still
Are on their way to worship at the temple on the hill.
Then if you look towards the sea, you'll see the longboats manned
By W'Lencing's men, the Saxons, who settled on this land.

Can you hear the sound of digging, turn your head, the straw is well
Is wellTrampled in the muddy surface for the dewpond in the dell.
Water that for generations served both animal and man
And though allowed to disappear, has been restored again.

Wagons up the hillside, men with pick and spade
Plant trees upon the summit and the Lancing Ring is made,
Locals called it Lancing Clump for a century or more,
And stories of its haunted past belong to Sussex lore.

The only people on the down in nineteen-forty-four
Are serving in the army, for England is at war.
A searchlight from the gun site picks out a German plane.
Is George, who used to live here, protecting us again?

The air is full of torment, as trees, torn from the ground
By winds of high velocity, fall groaning to teh ground.
The Lancing Ring lies beaten in the early morning light
But the many Friends of Lancing Ring come by to make it right.

Conn Gardner

A SUSSEX FISHERMAN'S ODE TO THE SEA

Our life is the sea
The sea is our living
Treat her with respect
And she'll do all the giving

Oh worship the sea
As she booms and she roars
Feel her tugging and pulling
Around at our oars

The sea is a Queen
With love as a parent's
She cares and admonishes
Bow down and give thanks!

We lowly meek men
Often despair.
To this lady of green
We can never compare.

Talya Bagwell

LOTTERY MANIA

In these days of fame and wealth
We could all be millionaires
But should that day somehow arrive who would be left who cares
For money does not count for much as we see more and more each day
That many who have won so much would gladly give it all away
If we sit down and study what we really need to live
We find that it's not what we take but rather what we give
Happiness we cannot buy but is there for all to share
It's being content with what we have and learning how to care
We need some money to survive and settle all the bills
But so many have more than they need and hope it will cure their ills
Good health is invaluable and does not need much giving
But can be helped by everyone with very careful living
So if we are blessed in this respect a windfall could be a curse
For if we seek an easy life fortune could make things worse
We could forget what life's about and end up like the rest
We'll not be remembered for what we had but the things that we did best
So should you join the ranks to win a lottery treasure
Do not be disillusioned if it don't bring instant pleasure
For we are born into this world with neither wealth nor fame
And despite what might seem good fortune we will all depart the same.

Reg Morris

HIGH SUSSEX

Along the Sussex South Downs way
Walks a Sussex South Down man.
As much a part of the land he treads,
As evolution's plan.

As timeless as the rolling chalk,
And the lark on the wind blown sky.
With the freedom of the turf to walk
In the magic of July.

Looking north, across the Weald,
As the Romans must have done,
The heat haze turns the land to smoke
In the warming, morning sun.

To the south, the gleaming sea,
As liquid silver lace.
To keep a continental chill at bay,
And to shape an island race.

From river Arun's long meander,
To swift ebbing Adur's flow,
The beauty of the county
Is there for all to know.

The Romans and the Saxons,
Left a cherished history,
From Bignor, Sompting, Bramber,
On to Norman Pevencey.

So walk the Sussex high ground,
Give your soul a splendid lift.
Forget the troubles of a modern world
And embrace true nature's gift.

E W Tomkins

GRANGE COURT DRIVE

No avenue of stately trees,
No mansions tall and grand,
Yet ev'rything there was to please,
And all was close at hand.

The gardens were a joy to spy,
With flowers bright and gay,
On winter branches 'gainst the sky,
And bush where berries lay.

The beauty of the woods was near,
With ever-changing trees;
The varied skies, now dull, now clear;
So much on which to muse!

For easy access to a shop,
Just through the *Twittons* walk;
Here one would often want to stop,
And with one's friends to talk.

What was the magic of the street?
'Twas not the homes so good,
But friendly neighbours who would meet
Just where and when they could.

Our homes, of course they were our own,
And yet in time of need,
We knew we only had to phone
To find a friend indeed.

Joy Kerton

MY COUNTRYSIDE

In the sky there are doves,
In the ground there are shrubs.
The breeze is blowing on to you.
On the grass there is dew.
In the long grass rabbits run,
What's that light it's the sun.
On the hill there is more than one daisy,
And the field looks very hazy.
In the field there are lots of wild flowers,
Rabbits stay there for hours and hours.

Gemma Butler (11)

SANCTUARY IN A SOUTH-EAST CITY

The waking day demands that news
And music must invade our home;
Factory, shop and office
Add their clamour : Childrens' boisterous
Bedlam, each yelling their way to school.

The noisy train, taking the strain,
Competes for racket with the plane,
Or helicopter prattle.
Walkmans, though miniature their scale,
Saw at senses like mosquitoes' whine.

Summer's curse - the open window
Spewing forth loud Radio Moron's
Arrogant irruption;
Conurbation's discord drowning
Opposition to the cult of noise.

It seems that nature's cherished gifts
Are rarely to be found within
A city's boundary;
Beauty and *silence* - and of these,
Sweet silence, the last to be conserved.

Yet beauty is within these walls
Of Canterbury: blessed peace
Cathedral doors enclose.
Decibels of commerce silenced;
Calmed, the daily round, the common task.

This city's holy sanctuary
Gives our minds the chance to breathe the
Purity of silence.
The stillness, not a muffling mute,
But an oxygen, restoring life!

Don Reeve

A BUFFER OF LEAFY GREEN

The place where I live is caught in a time warp 'twixt suburbia and
open land.
One side cramped and crowded, the other spacious and grand.
We seem to be like a boundary, a buffer in between,
the storming charge of progress and the walk of leafy green.
It's a shame to see the coloured fields all disappear from view,
as hedgerows and grassland is chopped up and broken into.
Suburbia's march on the countryside increases through the years.
and only those that remember will shed some quiet tears.
For future generations will not know what once had been,
instead of cramped suburbia it was spacious leafy green.
So hope that little buffer resists the pressure to melt,
into a rushing suburbia, taking with it our children's greenbelt.

Linda M Vincent

TWO HATS

Living in the South East's great
There is no doubt of that

But if you decide to move out here
Be prepared to wear two hats

There's many a quiet spot to be found
The sea and salty air

With villages, the downs and streams
And blossoms everywhere

But, the South East has another side
It's competitive and strong

With rush and bustle, push 'n' shove
And there are many who do long

To escape the race, the hectic pace
And leave the hustling throng

But they know without doubt
There's an easy way out

As they hastily retreat
To their cottages in the countryside
Where everything's so neat

So when you come to the South East
Don't forget you'll need two hats

One to wear in the countryside
And one 'mongst the high rise flats.

Helen Babette Lisney

45

WEST GRINSTEAD 1939

I see again with childhood's eye,
Especially now old age draws nigh,
The scenes that in my memory live,
And are evermore evocative,
Return to times in West Grinstead
And a way of life that now has fled.
Vincent Galsworthy, half-brother of John,
Owned *The Lodge*, and ordered on
No account to speak of him,
As he was a profligate *Bohemian*!
In other matters, though, he was
A gentle, courteous man, because
He invited friends to stay
To avoid the War's affray.
Nearby, the Catholic Presbytery,
Ran the *Boy's Reformatory*
As a house of correction
For those guilty of dereliction
Of the law. Oftimes, miscreants,
Because of disobedience,
Had to run behind a master
Cycling uphill, ever faster,
To make the lad learn his lesson
And turn him into a better person.
Near the station was the general shop,
An Aladdin's cave in which to stop,
While the school at Partridge Green,
Catered for the pupils keen.
But I'm afraid time's ta'en its toll,
There's hardly anything left at all!

B Gordon

WINTER IN THE GARDEN OF ENGLAND

I sit by my window
The rain pouring down
You would think it would make
One scowl and frown.
If I sit very quiet I know I will be
Warmed by the picture in front of me.

Little Robin Red Breast
Hops down the path
He came for the tit-bits
I put on the grass.

The handsome bold blackbird
With bright yellow beak
Is searching the bushes
For something to eat.

After he's eaten, I know where he'll be
In the pond
Splashing with glee.

Sheila Clifford

DARTFORD 1995

It was raining again today, isn't that always the way
When you're sitting there, planning your escape!
This place can be a prison cell, and the children make it hell
Nothing else to do but sit and watch the rain!
I walked along to Wilmot Park, dragged the children, and the cart,
Only when we got there it was drowning too!
Bricks and stones broken in half, how can they call this mess a path?
Alexander nearly lost a tooth!
If only there was a nursery, that I could send the kids for free!
A place that's near enough for little legs to walk.
Then I wouldn't feel the strain, or the monetary drain,
Or the guilt of what my children miss each day.

Sixty-eight pounds, thirty pee! This is what they think of me.
Future children of a generation, don't even get nursery education
Unless they're battered, abused, neglected, or financially selected
Someone tell me, please, is this my destiny?

This is England's countryside, yet there's one thing you can't hide,
Alexander's asthma's getting worse again!
His little body lay so still, how can my child be so ill?
In the place they call the garden of our land.
It's four thirty in the morning, uncontrollably I'm wailing,
I'm so scared each time I see him in this state.
Five days later we come home, why do I feel so alone,
Trapped by his nebuliser twice a day.
I guess you'd call this modern life, single mothers now are rife,
Only having kids for what they can get, they say.
Well I haven't got a council house, and I live from hand to mouth,
For the children that I couldn't give away!

Claire Lauren McAllen

48

SUSSEX BY THE SEA

Sussex born and Sussex bred,
Strong in the arm, weak in the head.
I am not silly, you will agree.
Living here beside the sea.

With lovely countryside close by
See grazing cows and sheep.
Ears of corn dance in the breeze.
The wildlife is asleep.

Or one day I can paddle
In the shiny glistening sea.
Visit the castles and museums
And eat fish and chips for tea.

A walk to view the lighthouse,
Our county's famous for.
Or down below the chalky cliff
The rock pools on the shore.

Why don't you pay a visit
To Sussex by the sea.
There is plenty going on here.
For folks like you and me.

Patricia Taylor

WILD SWANS

I saw wild swans
Swoop in and weave
Like shuttles on
The threadbare winter scene

With piercing cries
On whistling wind
They needled through
The faded tapestry
Of thorn and swollen stream

And made me wonder
Were it sign
Of winter's grey demise

Foretaste of spring's
Much softer touch
That played with light
For younger shoots to shine

Though slow to soar
And lifting gradually
They stirred strange hope
Those wild love birds

Still chasing faithfully
Across the years
And warmed the heart
To think of spring's surprise.

Rosemary Keith

MILL HILL SUMMER 1994

The South Downs behind Shoreham
Can be seen from miles away,
How fine the view from Mill Hill
On a clear and sunny day.

In the distance Shoreham Airport
Awakening memories galore,
Thriving still, amongst our oldest
Valued both in peace and war.

The years dissolve, we're climbing high
In a Beagle Pup no less,
The river Adur curves and holds
My heart in silent happiness.

And now a vibrant hum surrounds me,
Nearby strives an earnest group
Of men and boys manipulating
Model planes to loop the loop.

The old tollbridge seems peaceful now,
No longer needs to bear the strain
Of endless noisy, heavy traffic
Gone to the motorway fast lane.

Glancing right and straight ahead,
Stands Lancing College sure and bold,
The chapel in its timeless beauty
Enthralling me as I behold.

This part of Sussex like a friend,
Has long endeared itself to me,
The gentle Downs, the bluebell woods,
And never far away, the sea.

M Eyres

OUR VILLAGE

Not everyone lives in a village near sea
So well loved by history
Where King John granted a charter
For a street market to be held thereafter.

A lovely old church with crooked steeple
From where the bells ring in the people
Where many couples choose to marry
For photos at the lychgate tarry.

Where Thomas Becket spent a night
In Bishop's Palace before his plight
Of losing his head in Canterbury
No wonder he could not feel too merry.

Walk to a garden just to view
Fig trees bearing - not one or two
A high tower stands behind in glory
It puzzles me, what is the story?

Our post office is a busy store
Some items pile up from the floor
It also is a meeting place
To exchange news with a friendly face

Tomatoes were grown here by the score
Lovely flavoured ones - and more
But the need for houses and roads
Meant greenhouses were demolished in loads.

Where is this place we are proud to live
Which over the years had much to give
It is West Tarring - near Worthing and flowers
Do pay us a visit in sunshine or showers.

O E McShee

THOUGHTS OF SUMMER

Walking down a country lane
Trees budding incandescently profane
I thought of barmy summer days ahead.

Birds chirping through the forest dense
Bluebells shaking their merry bells hence
Of rivers flowing languidly in depths of murky green
And mother swans with their cygnets proudly seen
Gliding along with less cares than I
Who can only look on whilst breathing a sigh.

For all the glory of a summer's day
Peaceful and harmonious I watch as I lay
Down in the meadow green where no eyes can pry
No better place the wind whispering nigh
Than God's green earth this land. This England
So fair and abundantly grown
In nature's chest her treasures shown.

To rich and poor alike no distinction there
A kaleidoscope of colour, in birds of the air
Trees tall and shapely to shade us we share
Whilst the skies to affinity laid bare.

Jackie Oung

THE LIFEGUARD

You will glance across at me, but never see,
The woman that's inside of me.
My thoughts, my feelings, quite erotic,
The blush upon my cheek
Is not the flush of middle age
But more likened to a beast within a cage.

Your body looks so slim and taut,
Hair dark and thick, your eyes a haunting blue.
You're quite the dishiest man I've seen,
I picture scenes . . . Which I wish could be true,
Now they are dashed
Here comes your company . . .
A Baywatch double, not an old Gran like me!

Barbara Morris

THE BATTLE OF JOYDEN'S WOOD

There is war is our back garden, the wild life's *very* wild,
Relations have reached an all-time low twixt Man and beast and child,
The battle's long and bloody - Nature's red in tooth and claw,
We don't need to read the newspapers to get our share of war.
The squirrels tried it first with a subtle, quiet invasion
Nesting in our chimney was their form of peaceful persuasion.
Then, once routed from their nest, they decided to get tough
Pillaging the bluetit's nuts; as if that wasn't enough
A heron now regards our pond as a gourmet restaurant;
It contains all the favourite dishes that he could ever want.
Now the robin's a bit of a bully, his table manners are rude
Chasing other birds from the table, so that he gets all the food.
The magpies remind me of vikings, raiding along the shore,
Carrying away baby blackbirds, clasped squealing in their claw.
They can do what they want to each other; I really don't care how or why-
It's when they start on *me* that I sound my battle-cry.
Some bees built a nest in a vent in my loo one day,
Trying to add to their empire - so I gave them a spray
But the mice took the biscuit (I won't repeat what we said)
A whole platoon of them were billeted in a mattress in our shed!
Now, all's fair in love and war: we'll give nature a chance:
Hang on - hand me the pellets; those *bloody* snails are eating my best
                                                                plants!

Rosemary Champion

THROUGH THE WINDOW

I used to look through my window and I could see,
Green grass blowing in the wind,
Trees so high reaching to a blue sky
Birds singing flying high,
My heart was lifted for the day,
How lucky I am to see this on a beautiful day.
Now I see roofs of houses and rubbish around,
Concrete here concrete there - it seems to be everywhere
In the tree were tall birds,
Flying in and out in their glee
Now I look the trees have all been cut down
Beech and oaks are dead in the ground.

K E Clarke

THE TARMAC AND THE GRIT

Our road, you know is going grey
Like many others as it goes,
Shiny once the rain has gone and quilted when it snows.
Ask me, go on ask me,
To draw a plan of all the holes-
Not just drains where pennies fell
But where we made our football goals.
Even curbs might look like just a bit where pushchairs can't quite go,
But once on hands and knees you see
It's there the ebb of childhoods flow.
And whilst I might remember still
The patterns that my curtains made,
The tarmac and the grit outside
Is where my favourite games were played.

Matthew Herbert

BRIGHTON BELLE

Seagulls say it all,
Brazen cacophony, their raucous call,
It's seaside and sunshine, and sarnies by the sea,
A walk on the pier, and fish and chips for tea,
A tattoo or a tarot card, you can see a seal or two,
Madame Tusaud's wonderful, to bring out the ghoul in you.
A pint along the promenade, a pie and peas for two
(By now you'll need a toilet, Pavilion gardens here will do)
Pubs and pizzas, pies and pastas,
A veritable haven, of goldsmiths and of galleries,
In the lanes are close to hand,
So is the Pavilion, Prince Regent made so grand.
Go, for a day, for a week,
Go and have a ball, the seagulls say it all.

Jane Wilmshurst

A HAVEN AT CUCKMERE

Glistening in the breezy cool,
Ripples on the water, like trinkets of shiny blue.
High tides, boats a wavering,
Seaweed drifting, swimmers bathing,

Net dipping on river edge,
Kite flying overhead.
Ramblers walking to the shore;
Ice-cream van putting smiles on faces,
Sticky hands galore.

Light engine plane trails into the distance
What a beautiful day, makes life worth its existence.
Kestrel hovering on the wind; rabbits dart about,
Nature is whole; then disappears quickly, all for a child's shout.

Cascades of brilliant sunlight dance; as you walk.
On winding path; beside the chalk.

Gate, pond, then manmade road to Fox Hole Farm,
Watch a sheepdog demonstration, then a living exhibition,
Sheering and weaving in the barn.

Pill boxes scattered, derelict and empty,
Different from the days of war when they mattered,
Compared to today's world of plenty.

River meandering down to the sea.
Shoes threading pebbles; hard and abrasive,
Waves lapping rocks; in pools - mussels and limpets exposed

Headed with seaweed, slimy and green.
Crabs, blennys, prawns, and anemone; a world evasive,
To be found and seen.

Walk back, via the track,
Dusk says 'We're finished our stay, come back again,
And enjoy another of Nature's Day.'

Stephanie Rose

LANCING THE GOLDEN

Lancing! Oh Lancing! Pearl of the south
(Please don't ridicule as the words leave my mouth)
We have so much to offer, so much to delight
(Admittedly, there's not much to do here at night)
But we have several pubs, and the library's a winner,
But the latter's closed at 7.00, so if you're a swinger
You could try the Legion or the Empire Club,
Or adult education, which is often at the hub
Of activities hereabouts, and then culture is alive and well
At the M.A.D.D. theatre - their shows are really swell.
The theatre itself is small, but thriving,
(Husband Jon, and daughter Tegan begged this advertising)
They belong to the company - a busy, happy band
New members always welcome - to act or lend a hand.
But if sport's your thing, there's the leisure centre,
A place of vim and vigour - I seldom ever venture
Within its walls! - and then there's the beach
At low tide this is smooth and sandy
But mostly it's quite pebbly, which again is handy
As you wouldn't want to sit and fry in the sun
Much better to jump up, and go for a run
On Beach Green itself or even up to Lancing Clump
(Supported by conservationists and now devoid of junk)
Alright, Lancing isn't perfect (or even close!)
But it's just the place for a bracing dose
Of sea air, and I'm sure you would find
There's nothing quite like village life to broaden the mind!

Helen French

STARK REALITY

The green of our country retreats,
As an ugly road rears its head,
More cars, more fumes our air secretes,
Unfortunate hedgehog, a victim lies dead.

Passionless people don't seem to care,
Wrapped up in money, eternal greed,
Wagers and lotteries, a jolly fare,
The root of all evil plants its seed.

A homeless poor man begs for change,
While drunken yobs smash and rampage,
The old live in fear, it isn't so strange,
That society robs in this new age.

A chink of light in the grey sky,
Falls on our town, to start a new day,
As those who govern continue to lie,
Our hope lives on in its red ray.

R M West

THE DARENT IN FLOOD

The river Darent in January flood
Burst its banks to create shimmering lakes
Where before lay meadows of mud.
So gazing down, from rainsoaked hills,
Where in clay and chalk I tread,
I saw the lakes like a string of jewels
Joined by the rivers silver thread.
Though my soul still weeps for that autumn night
When a million beeches fell,
And when the plague took all the elms
It took part of me as well.
On my valleys steep side I stop for breath and muse.
It was those past cruel clearances
That made way for today's fine views.
So flood havoc you winter river
Go not quietly to the sea
Wash away those prophets of the summer drought
Who said we'd seen the end of you.
Forgive my summer sorrow as I walked on your dried stones,
I believed that you had gone for good
And I was walking on your bones.

M Fittock

UNTITLED

Arundel is beautiful,
Littlehampton's fine.
But Wick, I guess,
Is best of all.
I s'pose because it's mine.

It might not be Regent Street
Hyde Park or Leicester Square.
But Wick, I guess,
Is best of all.
I s'pose because we're there.

Anything you want to buy
Is there, it's not too dear.
For Wick, I guess,
Is best of all.
I s'pose because it's near.

Wick people aren't stand-offish,
Don't treat you cold as ice.
So Wick, I guess,
Is best of all.
I s'pose because it's nice.

Wick's got houses, pubs and shops,
Far as the eye can roam.
You want to know
What's best of all?
I s'pose, because Wick's home.

Lynda Shaw

'SUPER MARE

Down from *Brum* to see the sea
But my oh! my, where can it be?
Just muddy shores and donkey rides
Boats lying idly on their sides,
A noisy pier and barking dogs
Tell tale feet of muddy bogs.
Ponies running round in circles
Children's voices full of chortles.
It's noisy, muddy but oh, the air.
I love it here in 'Super Mare.

No more holidays here for me,
In Super Mare where there's no sea.
It's not the dogs or noisy pier
Why I won't come on holiday here.
The simple fact is this you see
I chose to live here permanently.
I live here now without a care
And breathe in deeply, lovely air
So come on down, just find the fare
Come to lovely 'Super Mare.

R L Youster

WINTER BLUES

Another wet morning for Dartford Heath.
I put on my wellies and gritted my teeth.
In no way daunted I set about my daily venture
To take out the dog for his usual adventure.

Walking our pets, both big and small.
The same routine goes for us all.
The familiar faces, damp and cold
Our pets up front, excited and bold

We must be mad we say as we pass
This really is no drawing room farce.
But, if we are honest, we must confess.
We would not miss our walks despite the mess.

The heathland might be cold and wet just now
But spring is coming and the buds are on the bough.
Soon the gorse will show its yellow cloak
And winter will fade for us doggy folk.

The mud will dry with the strong March winds
So that we shall lose our fish-like fins
And what pleasure we shall all derive
From how good it feels just to be alive.

To walk our pets in woodland places
Sporting a healthy glow upon our faces.
Yes! winter passes into verdant spring
And walking the dog is just the thing!

Iris Sheridan

THE CHOICE IS KENT

There's nothing like life
In south east Kent
I once heard
From an elderly gent

Either fast or slow
The pace is yours
The young run around
The elderly explore

The choice is here
For the lifestyle you lead
Either quiet or busy
Kent has all you need

The variety is endless
From a lane to a street
But all have grass, trees and flowers
And places to meet

Where else would you live
But on Kentish ground
Where you are close to a village
But not far from a town?

Lindsay Lewis-Ranwell

IS SOME DOLLY BIRD SHIELDING YOU?

Does your conscience prick at night in bed,
Do you toss from side to side
Do you wake up screaming from your sleep,
Remembering that sad night.
Claire Tiltman was in the prime of life
Her loving parents pride and joy
Until you murderer came along,
And left her there to die.

Do you walk 'round now in a daze,
Are drugs your only cure
Your only cure to forget that night,
You no good son of a whore.
Is your GP. at wits end with you,
Trying to mend your loony brain
Trying to mend the brain of a murderer,
That's inflicted so much pain.

So come forward now Count Dracula,
No good member of mankind
Before your bloody hand will strike again,
When an innocent child you will find.
Is some dolly bird shielding you,
Shielding you day and night
Ever since you murdered lovely Claire,
In that alley-way at Greenhithe.

James Prendeville

LAMENT FOR LANCING

People don't seem to share any more
Their lives are like boarded up shops
Each one behind their own door
Fastened by chains, bolts and locks.

With bells ringing and flashing red light
The trains rattle through, rarely stopping.
The buses don't run much at night
And we're forced out of town for our shopping.

Where once you'd buy shoes, hats, a bed
Or fresh fish and veggies a'plenty,
Now the centre is practically dead
With more and more shops standing empty.

New roads will cut downland in two
But the pavement's in need of repairing
The sea water's not good for you
No wonder I'm near to despairing!

Things surely can't get any worse
Here's hoping they'll soon be much better.
I've had my say penning this verse
Now I'm writing my MP a letter.

Pat Izod

CONFRONTING REALITY

I saw you sitting there in Canterbury
Tonight
'Any change please? Any change?'
I walked on by
I walked on by
Consumed with guilt now
But it is too late
I already walked on by
You do not need these selfish tears
You do not need to see me cry
What you need I did not give
I walked on by
I have just watched the screenplay on BBC2
I saw others - even children
Just like you
Tonight
I saw
Ugliness - the system which justifies
The way it treats you
I always thought that
Life was my life
I always thought that
Everyone
Lived in the same way as me
Loved, cared for, spoilt and free
I just could not see any further
Than my own reality
Daddy always tells me
How fortunate I am
How some children starve
How some babies die
How some adults despair
How some parents never care
But I just could not see

More than the words

The Words

But tonight you changed all that

Tonight I saw
The
Reality

Amanda Hewett

RETIREMENT

We moved house last summer
From a big house by the sea
Four bedrooms and three bathrooms
Much too large for you and me.
Grandchildren came for holidays,
Grew up happily and free,
In the big house with four bedrooms
Much too large for you and me.
We now live in the country
In a nice secluded spot.
Fields and sheep and horses
Now make up our happy lot
We no longer have to face the wind
Or battle with the sea,
In our bright and shining bungalow
That's just right for you and me.

Josephine Ann Anderson

GRANDSON'S DAY OUT

The car's all packed, we're off out,
That's what today is all about.
On the brow of the hill we look down,
Golden corn, radiant, all around.
The grey contrast of a church's spire,
Tall and proud in its cool green shroud.
Not long now to find the river,
To count the ducks, sticklebacks and minnows.
Through the ford to the other side (and back again to keep him quiet).
The highland cows have gone away,
No more shaggy calves at play.
The viaduct remains with its elegant arches-
We'll wave at a train as it passes.
Swallows swoop, warblers sing,
Summer time in Eynsford, such a precious thing.

Charlotte White

THE POWER AND THE GLORY

Fire to warm us in the cold
Earth to hold us strong and bold,
Air to breathe and give us life
Water flowing day and night.

Planets, stars, moon and sun
Light and beauty every one,
Within the earth deep and dark
Turned to coal lie trees and bark.

Silver, copper, iron and gold
Men have dug since days of old,
Precious stones of varied hue
Green and yellow, red and blue.

Man and creatures, plants and trees
God our Father made all these,
And when the time on earth was right
Jesus came on Christmas night.

Margaret Gibian

WACKY RACES

They've gone and ruined all our fun,
Since supermarkets first began
Trolleys built to cruise the aisles
Were freed to roam for miles and miles

Closing time brought one desire
To ride that chariot of Wire
Inebriated, but stout of heart
They're Ben Hur in a shopping cart

To the clock tower brave charioteers!
Full of gassy German beers.
With wheels that leave you in the lurch,
While cornering by the Catholic church.

You didn't need your social graces,
To join in Gravesend's wacky races.
But no longer can be heard,
The crunch of wheels upon the kerb

Gravesend council's had their way
And trolley racing's had its day,
Now the drunks of Gravesend weep,
And cruise the town upon their feet.

Alison Hazel

CLEVEDON PROMENADE

Beached by time
Behind this Victorian window I watch
Rain in trembling threads cross glass
Bending far-off rainbowed sails
A pale sun filters through billowing clouds
Fists of birds unfurl, wheel skywards
Across the slender finger of sculptured pier
Anglers' lines flash and whip into flaked slate sea
Tangled blossoms of seaweed dress the shore
Rosy pebbles sought as treasures to paint
Or thrown as skimming missiles through foam.
Children burst from cars slamming doors
Their chatter echoes like a shell to my ears
With arms full of towels, picnics and crabbing tackle
They rush for the slipway, bind bread on hooks
Skittering crabs wave amber pincers, scissoring air
To squeals of delight
Parents read, musing quietly
Then buy snowy mountains of ice-creams
That drip through clamorous hands onto smiling lips
Morning slips through a net of slow memories
As smoothly as lovers that pace along poet's Walk
Sheltering for kisses under trees bent double by scything winds
Their pleasure as sharp as the cat
Stalking the wary blackbird beyond
This pane.

Melanie Greenwood

NEVER TO BE MISSED

You can travel the world and never see such sights,
As the crisp Kentish mornings and the star shining nights.
To be awoken each day with the bird's joyful song,
Walk the long winding lanes that forever go on.
It is life at its finest, not to be missed.
If you've not been here yet, put Kent on your list.

Pamela Creaven

THE GAMEKEEPER'S TREE

Stoats and weasels dripping with dew
Are strung up there for all to view
Shattered with lead from a ruthless gun
Never to know what became of their young

An old barn owl hangs up high
A wise bird who once ruled the night sky
Then his eyes were big and bright
Now sunken, dull, a dreadful sight

He's even crucified the poor old mole
A velvet coated gentleman that lived down a hole
Maggots fall earthwards from the carcass of a rat
Only one life for him, not nine like the cat

A Rooks' ebony feathers spiral in the warm summer breeze
Whilst his flock defiantly caw in the distant elm trees
On the ground below the corpses decay and smell
To any passing animal this *tree* must signify *hell*.

Clive Gravett

ARUNDEL IN MARCH

She sits below the Arbutus,
Your lady love with letter.
Your beauteous words give her delight
But hearing you would be better.
Perhaps in May you both will share
The bench which she did find.
Then she can say *'Thank you my dear*
For gifts of every kind.'
Your poems, art and chocolates too
Are all sent from your heart.
She like to share them all with you
And never grow apart.
So, gallant knight, review her there
And Arundel will be more fair.

Francesca R Winson

SOUND SCULPTURE

Soothing sea
Sounds in the ear;
Brushing, sweeping,
Whispering against the eardrum
Like a feather palpitating with life.
A candle's flame is like this also
And the waters creep in
Like light night.

Fragile as a snail-shell,
Rolling love between two insubstantial fingers,
Contemplative,
Establishing the high tide mark
And time.

Carefully. Caressingly.
The sea runs its finger
Up and over the sand's spine,
Hitting nerves
And causing shivers.

Delicate as the fragile ear hammer
Is love; and the sea is this also.
The little drum-beats inside the head
Increase when the waves sigh,
Spelling out the words that seem to say
Small, small,
And beautiful am I.

Duncan Chappell

THE PHOTOGRAPH

Snap - the shutter closes - image caught
And placed upon the mantel - silver frame
Takes pride of place. Victorian she stands,
Within an antique treasure - never mind her name.

A subject for discussion, water-coloured in.
'Is that sky blue, or just an azure grey?
Of course, that must be Henley, can you see the boats?
Another drink? It doesn't matter anyway.'

They turn their backs; but still she smiles,
At one who loved her and would always keep,
That time at Bognor on their one day off,
When they held hands and walked along the beach.

Elizabeth Cahillane

BURPHAM

Timeless cricket on the village green;
And all around the sound of bees.
Across the vale the castle stands
Like a galleon sailing the seven seas.
And Nature's potent magic sends
The wild flower scents on the summer breeze.

The George and Dragon, Burpham's inn,
A meeting place for young and old.
Were smugglers spoils divided here
And many a thrilling story told.
Did men who lived a double life
Come here to spend their hard-won gold.

Over her flock, St Mary's church
Stands guard, a watchful eye to keep.
And in the churchyard, all at peace
So many generations sleep.
What spot more tranquil could there be
For those bereaved to stand and weep.

Take now the lane to Peppering;
The farm with wondrous views is blessed.
Of field and river, hills and park
And raucous crows flying home to nest.
To crown it all, the wondrous sight
Of a golden sun sinking down in the west.

At High Barn now look over the fields
To see the path the lepers trod,
From lonely downland settlements
So poorly clothed and roughly shod.
To gaze through the window of their church
Denied the presence of their God.

Tony Malone

GLORIOUS GOODWOOD

Ahh! Glorious Goodwood
'Tis for some
I wish I had the money
To go and see them run!

Spot the Roller, the Bentley
And don't forget the Porsche,
You'll find them scattered
All over the course.

The thunder of hooves,
Power in time,
Plough up the turf
As they race for the line.

Hands in the air,
We've just bred a winner,
Find extra staff
There's a hundred for dinner!

Champers and lobster,
Punter and tipster,
Ahh! Glorious Goodwood,
'Tis for some.

Kings and Queens
Have graced the turf
Everything in life
Leads back to the earth!

Derrick Evers

THOUGHTS OF A WORTHING METAL DETECTIVE

The day I see an angler reel in and land a kipper,
Or I listen to the local Sally Army play *The Stripper,*
When the pavement cycling regulations cease to knock on wood,
And the seagulls all behave and drop their blessings where they should-

And the day I see the Jolly Roger flying at the Pier,
And no creature put at risk by disregarded fishing gear,
When graffitists turn out murals like Rivera at his best,
And the price of litter on the beach exceeds a treasure chest-

And the day that this contraption here starts giving out vibrations
That will spread themselves throughout the world and bring peace
                                                      unto nations-
Yes, the day all these things happen will be when my dreams unfold;
Because that will be the day that I'll have found my crock of gold.

Stephen Rudgwick

THE STONES SHALL RISE UP

The Midnight Rambler roamed these streets
Where Shelley and Mary stopped far eats.
When Henry got tired of his fourth Greensleeves
Our Nunnery sheltered Anne of Cleves.
In music we've never gone for wrong
We have the warbler and his own, sweet song.
Trevithick steamed on with deep devotion
Years ahead with his locomotion.
Marshall made machines to watermark
And helped to print money for a lark.
Boroughs wellcome found out about insulin
Followed up smartly with Digoxin.
If the county planners have their way
Dear old Dartford has had its day.
But the spirit of Tyler will linger on
Long after the planners and plotters have gone.

Shelagh Shannon

HOLIDAYS AT WHITSTABLE

In the days of long ago,
Sometime after the war,
My family and I would make our way,
To Whitstable and its shores.
The beach was always crowded,
We had a job to park,
But my family would converge there,
For a weekends fun and lark.
Grandad owned a chalet,
Up on the grassy slopes,
Nan would serve up cups of tea
And welcome us with her best brew.
So life was good and happy
With the family we loved and knew.
At night we'd sleep upon the beach,
Twenty-two of us, in two lines neat,
Beneath the stars and warm soft breeze,
And sound of surf lapping near our feet.
The hours would pass by peaceably,
No-one knew we were there,
The weekends were so happy
We had no single care.
We cockled in the sandy pools,
And winkled in the sand.
We sat and heard the war tales,
From my uncles and my dad.
Of how they fought and won the war
To preserve our land.
Life was very happy then.
So simple, not so grand.

Janet Smart

THE KESTREL

Iron-grey, angry October sea;
Swirling steely clouds above me;
The stark white bones of chalk track unwinding beneath my feet.
At a barred gate I pause and rest:
In a rotted hollow atop a wooden post,
Scattered, small balls of feather, fur and bone:
A Kestrels egesta.
I run on, searching the sombre sky for his petrified silhouette.
There! High! Riding the wind, laying on the breeze
As though suspended by an invisible thread to the clouds above.
To his hawk eyes, the tapestry of downs below, shows life,
Unseen to my myopic human vision.
The autumn shorn fields provide scant cover for his small prey;
The tiny lives, scamper and flit across the shaven pate of stubbled acres,
Whose cropped, flaxen head of corn and barley and wheat,
Lies stored, safe now in farmers barn.
The melanaemic, burnt adjacent fields,
Blackened gums in agéd autumn's face,
Give even less protection.
I run on, the oily stench of this Aceldama in my nostrils
Conjures a dream of these same southern downs,
Fleshed with their sleek, golden, summer curves;
A sun-kissed, taut-skinned, enticing Goddess.
Now! He stoops! A high pitched squeal reaches me;
One more death! A few more drops of blood in sacrifice to the earth.
I run on, morbid thoughts soon dispelled by the timeless hills.
The Kestrel, now behind me, soars up and takes station again,
Untouched and unshaken by the freshening southerly breeze;
And the thoughts of my own mortality.

Barry Rice

CONVALESCENCE (DOWNLAND RAMBLE)

Slowly, as the new sun lit the day,
And cool sea breezes shook the quaking grass,
We climbed a hill to overture of wren,
While fairy flax and cowslip lined our path.

In a Himalayan fantasy in miniature,
I was Hilary with Tensing at the pass.
Our spirits rose with every undulation
As we set to conquer Seven Sisters' hearts.

Now sheepish clouds hung loose from southern skies,
And followed one another to the north.
But, reddened by the devilish rising sun,
Resembled beings alien to the Earth.

I imagined labyrinths beneath our feet.
What secrets of our forbears could they tell?
Through hills that put all people in their place
I could almost hear a distant Saxon knell.

At length the mountains fell to Cuckmere Haven.
As we descended, the silent springy turf
Gave way to crunchy beach and cheering ocean
As pebbles danced with seaweed in the surf.

We left the line of misty hills behind.
The slowly setting sun fell from the weald.
A pause for quiet thoughts of deep contentment:
We'd walked away from illness and were healed.

Christopher Melhuish

DOVER

Come to Dover
Take the ferry and pop over
As the tourists do
They love it so
Why not go to the castle?
Get away from the hustle and bustle
Of every day worries
Or go to the *White Cliffs Experience*
And listen to the old stories
(Or to the museum)
Oh Dover!
We are proud of you over and over
So come to this ancient, busy and
Wonderful town
Don't let the cares and worries
Get you down.

S Coughlan

DRIVING TO WORK IN SUSSEX

How rich I was driving to work
Through such a wealth of memories and time.
On this corner the Abbott's cook
Dabbled in the stew-pond for a fat fish,
Hundreds of years ago
Where now the purple loose-strife pierce the slime.

On over the railway crossing next,
Across a small rough common, revealing where
The surprising vixen hunted
On my return at winter's dusk.
Mink face, mink brush, pale body,
- Hunger keeping her visible, with fixed and starving stare.

Now into the beauty of Littlington,
Each house cries out, a separate vibrant being.
Flowers cascade richly leaning down,
The aged yew sprawls on the church mound
Next to the ancient priory, facing
Far off, above strong scented violets, the Long Man, unseeing.

Up the slope to the turn!
The weald spreads out like an embroidered quilt.
My sense of time stands confused.
For where crow and hawk once looked down
On Saxon Alfred, riding past Saxon flax,
Now hang-gliders startle the eye as they hover, swoop and tilt.

So many delights tempt the gaze.
The powerful flight of swans compels the heart to throb.
Through clusters of bouncing lambs in spring
The Cuckmere's ox-bow loops to the far off sea
The departing ferry's hoot mourns the loss of Seven Sisters
And Sussex once again adds boundless wealth to my job.

Enid C King

INFORMATION

We hope you have enjoyed reading this book - and that you will continue to enjoy it in the coming years.

If you like reading and writing poetry drop us a line, or give us a call, and we'll send you a free information pack.

Write to

Anchor Books Information
1-2 Wainman Road
Woodston
Peterborough
PE2 7BU.